BASEBALL LEGENDS

Hank Aaron
Grover Cleveland Alexander
Ernie Banks
Johnny Bench
Yogi Berra
Roy Campanella
Roberto Clemente
Ty Cobb
Dizzy Dean
Joe DiMaggio
Bob Feller
Jimmie Foxx
Lou Gehrig
Bob Gibson
Rogers Hornsby
Reggie Jackson
Shoeless Joe Jackson
Walter Johnson
Sandy Koufax
Mickey Mantle
Christy Mathewson
Willie Mays
Stan Musial
Satchel Paige
Brooks Robinson
Frank Robinson
Jackie Robinson
Pete Rose
Babe Ruth
Nolan Ryan
Tom Seaver
Mike Schmidt
Duke Snider
Warren Spahn
Willie Stargell
Honus Wagner
Ted Williams
Carl Yastrzemski
Cy Young

CHELSEA HOUSE PUBLISHERS

BASEBALL LEGENDS

NOLAN RYAN

Lois P. Nicholson

Introduction by
Jim Murray
Member of the Baseball Hall of Fame

Senior Consultant
Earl Weaver

CHELSEA HOUSE PUBLISHERS
New York • Philadelphia

CHELSEA HOUSE PUBLISHERS

Editorial Director: Richard Rennert
Executive Managing Editor: Karyn Gullen Browne
Copy Chief: Robin James
Picture Editor: Adrian G. Allen
Creative Director: Robert Mitchell
Art Director: Joan Ferrigno
Production Manager: Sallye Scott

Baseball Legends

Senior Editor: Philip Koslow

Staff for NOLAN RYAN

Editorial Assistant: Scott D. Briggs
Designer: M. Cambraia Magalhães
Picture Researcher: Alan Gottlieb
Cover Illustration: Daniel O'Leary

3 5 7 9 8 6 4 2

Library of Congress Cataloging-in-Publication Data

Nicholson, Lois, 1949–
Nolan Ryan / Lois P. Nicholson.
p. cm   (Baseball legends)
Includes bibliographical references and index.
ISBN 0-7910-2174-2
1. Ryan, Nolan, 1947–   Juvenile literature. 2. Baseball players—
United States—Biography—Juvenile literature. [1. Ryan, Nolan,
1947– . 2. Baseball players.] I. Title. II. Series.
GV865.R9N53 1995   95-3099
796.357'092—dc20   CIP
[B]   AC

CONTENTS

WHAT MAKES A STAR

Jim Murray

No one has ever been able to explain to me the mysterious alchemy that makes one man a .350 hitter and another player, more or less identical in physical makeup, hard put to hit .200. You look at an Al Kaline, who played with the Detroit Tigers from 1953 to 1974. He was pale, stringy, almost poetic-looking. He always seemed to be struggling against a bad case of mononucleosis. But with a bat in his hands, he was King Kong. During his career, he hit 399 home runs, rapped out 3,007 hits, and compiled a .297 batting average.

Form isn't the reason. The first time anybody saw Roberto Clemente step into the batter's box for the Pittsburgh Pirates, the best guess was that Clemente would be back in Double A ball in a week. He had one foot in the bucket and held his bat at an awkward angle—he looked as though he couldn't hit an outside pitch. A lot of other ballplayers may have had a better-looking stance. Yet they never led the National League in hitting in four different years, the way Clemente did.

Not every ballplayer is born with the ability to hit a curveball. Nor is exceptional hand-eye coordination the key to heavy hitting. Big-league locker rooms are filled with players who have all the attributes, save one: discipline. Every baseball man can tell you a story about a pitcher who throws a ball faster than anyone has ever seen but who has no control on or *off* the field.

The Hall of Fame is full of people who transformed them-selves into great ballplayers by working at the sport, by studying the game, and making sacrifices. They're overachievers—and winners. If you want to find them, just watch the World Series. Or simply read about New York Yankee great Lou Gehrig; Ted Williams, "the Splendid Splinter" of the Boston Red Sox; or the Dodgers' strikeout king Sandy Koufax.

A pitcher *should* be able to win a lot of ballgames with a 98-miles-per-hour fastball. But what about the pitcher who wins 20 games a year with a fastball so slow that you can catch it with your teeth? Bob Feller of the Cleveland Indians got into the Hall of Fame with a blazing fastball that glowed in the dark. National League star Grover Cleveland Alexander got there with a pitch that took considerably longer to reach the plate; but when it did arrive, the pitch was exactly where Alexander wanted it to be—and the last place the batter expected it to be.

There are probably more players with exceptional ability who didn't make it to the major leagues than there are who did. A number of great hitters, bored with fielding practice, had to be dropped from their team because their home-run production didn't make up for their lapses in the field. And then there are players like Brooks Robinson of the Baltimore Orioles, who made himself into a human vacuum cleaner at third base because he knew that working hard to become an expert fielder would win him a job in the big leagues.

A star is not something that flashes through the sky. That's a comet. Or a meteor. A star is something you can steer ships by. It stays in place and gives off a steady glow; it is fixed, permanent. A star works at being a star.

And that's how you tell a star in baseball. He shows up night after night and takes pride in how brightly he shines. He's Willie Mays running so hard his hat keeps falling off; Ty Cobb sliding to stretch a single into a double; Lou Gehrig, after being fooled in his first two at-bats, belting the next pitch off the light tower because he's taken the time to study the pitcher. Stars never take themselves for granted. That's why they're stars.

1

"THIS IS UNHITTABLE"

Detroit Tigers pitcher Ed Farmer stood in the left-field bullpen at Tiger Stadium on the afternoon of July 15, 1973, watching the starting pitcher for the visiting California Angels warming up across the field. "I didn't think he was throwing very well," Farmer said later, "and then it dawned on me that he was 400 feet away from me, and I realized that he was throwing better than I had ever seen him."

The 26-year-old right-handed fireballer had come over to the American League the year before in a trade with the New York Mets and had immediately established himself as the most dominating and intimidating power pitcher in the game. He had led the league in strikeouts, walks, and scared hitters. Early in his second season, on May 15 in Kansas City, he had thrown his first no-hitter, striking out 12 in a 3–0 win.

But for all his overpowering stuff, Nolan Ryan's record stood at a modest 10 wins and 11 losses as he strode to the mound in Tiger

Nolan Ryan fires a fastball on July 15, 1973, en route to pitching a no-hitter against the Detroit Tigers. Ryan was to pitch a record total of seven no-hitters during the course of his phenomenal 27-year career.

Stadium on the night of July 15. Although he was giving up fewer than three earned runs per game, the Angels were giving him little support; they had the lowest team batting average and the second lowest run production in the league.

Ryan's first pitch on July 15 was supposed to be a fastball. But Ryan mistook the sign put down by the Angels catcher, Art Kusnyer (pronounced KUSH-ner), and threw a hard curve. The pitch sailed by Kusnyer and hit the umpire, Ron Luciano, on the knee.

"Get it right," growled Luciano, wincing in pain. The catcher and umpire looked at each other, sharing the same thought: anybody who can throw a curveball that hard to start the game has got the stuff to pitch a no-hitter.

The hitters soon had the same experience. They could barely see Ryan's fastball, much less put a bat on it. And they could only stare in frozen disbelief at the handful of wicked curves he broke off. As Detroit first baseman Norm Cash trudged back to the dugout after striking out in his first at-bat, he passed the next batter, Duke Sims.

"How's he throwing?" Sims asked.

"Don't go up there," Cash replied.

Ryan struck out 16 batters through the first seven innings. The Angels clung to a 1–0 lead until the eighth inning, when they erupted for five runs. Sitting on the bench during the extended half inning, Ryan felt his arm stiffen. When he took the mound for the bottom of the eighth, his fastball lost a little of its pop; he struck out only one of the last six batters. Still, only one ball was hit with any mustard on it, a line drive right at the shortstop with one out in the ninth. After the next out, Norm Cash loomed as Ryan's last challenge. As Cash stepped up to the plate, the bat he carried looked bigger than usual, and it was. After striking out twice, the Tigers slugger had gone into the clubhouse and taken a heavy wooden leg off a table. Now he was standing at the plate swinging it.

"Check his bat," Ryan hollered out to the umpire.

Luciano took the piece of lumber from Cash. "You can't bat with this old piano leg," he said. "Get rid of it."

"But I've got no chance with a bat," Cash pleaded. "Let me try this."

"Get rid of it," the umpire ordered.

Ryan could not help laughing as he watched; if he had felt any tension, the incident deflated it. He reared back and threw a fastball that Cash, now using a normal bat, popped up to the shortstop. Ryan thus became the fifth pitcher in baseball history to throw two no-hitters in a season.

Twenty years later, reflecting on a 45-year career in which he had seen more than 7,000 games, Tigers broadcaster Ernie Harwell singled out Ryan's July 15 no-hitter as the best-pitched game he ever saw. "You often hear the expression 'They were lucky to hit a foul ball off him,' " Harwell remarked. "That was completely true that afternoon. The Tigers were lucky to get a foul ball off Ryan."

"He was throwing close to 105 miles an hour," Ed Farmer estimated. "He was the most dominating I've ever seen a pitcher." Detroit outfielder Jim Northrup agreed. "We had no chance. He could have pitched 20 innings and we wouldn't have had a hit off him."

Four days later, Ryan almost became the first pitcher to throw three no-hitters in a year and

Followed by catcher Art Kusnyer, Ryan accepts congratulations from Angels manager Bobby Winkles after blanking the Tigers. Two months earlier, he had notched his first career no-hitter, establishing himself as one of baseball's most exciting performers.

the second to throw two in a row. He held the Baltimore Orioles hitless until the eighth inning. When Orioles hitter Terry Crowley drew a walk, he commented to Angels first baseman Mike Epstein, "I can't believe how hard Ryan's throwing. This is unhittable."

"He's five or six miles an hour slower than he was four days ago in Detroit," Epstein said.

Although many pitchers have turned in better won-lost records than Ryan's 21-16 in 1973, none has ever been more overpowering for a single season. In 23 of his 39 starts he struck out 10 or more. In his last start of the year, Ryan went 11 innings to beat Minnesota, 5–4, striking out 16. When he fanned Rich Reese for the final out, it was number 383 for the year, breaking the major league strikeout record set by Sandy Koufax of the Los Angeles Dodgers. Ryan would go on to pitch a total of seven no-hitters and break or tie 53 major league records, but claiming a record from his boyhood idol Koufax remained a highlight of his 27 years in the major leagues.

Just one year earlier, unable to control his fastball, Ryan had considered quitting baseball. But he had persevered, with long hours of practice and patient drilling by his coaches. Now the Ryan Express was roaring full throttle on the track to greatness.

2

ALVIN'S ACE PITCHER

Lynn Nolan Ryan, Jr., was born January 31, 1947, in Refugio, Texas, the sixth child of Lynn Nolan Ryan, Sr., and Martha Ryan. The family called the youngster Nolan to distinguish him from his father, whom everyone called Lynn. Six months after Nolan's birth, Lynn Ryan, an oil company supervisor, was transferred to his firm's plant at Hastings, 25 miles south of Houston. The Ryans moved to nearby Alvin, a town of 5,000 people where spreading oak trees lined peaceful streets.

The six Ryan children—Lynda, Mary Lou, Robert, Judy, Jean, and Nolan—packed the family's four-bedroom ranch house, but outside there was plenty of space. The town was surrounded by open fields where ranchers raised cattle and farmers grew rice. The flat landscape was dotted by oil wells that coaxed ink-black crude from the Texas earth.

In Alvin, as in many other American towns, baseball was an important part of the community's life. The preparation of the vacant lot near Nolan's home was a spring ritual. Air-conditioned homes were almost unheard of in that era, and many families did not own television sets. But no one thought of staying indoors. Even in the heat of a Texas summer, the kids

Nolan Ryan as a high school senior in 1965. Growing up in Alvin, Texas, young Nolan developed a passion for sports and a dedication to excellence.

played ball. "It was horribly hot and humid, but we didn't care until sometimes in the middle of the day when it was so hot you couldn't stand it out in the sun," recalled Nolan. "Then we'd lie around in the shade until it cooled down a few degrees and we could get back at it."

If he had no baseball, Nolan threw anything within reach. "My mother was always on me for breaking windows or hitting the car," he remembered. "I especially liked going down to Mustang Bayou near our house to throw rocks at the water moccasins and turtles." The family dog, a brown-and-white fox terrier named Suzy, followed him everywhere.

Lynn and Martha Ryan gave their children strong family values and a secure home. However, they did not indulge them with material things. With six children to raise, Lynn Ryan's salary was stretched to the limit. Nolan learned the value of a dollar at an early age. "When school started each year we'd go to the store and I'd get two pairs of jeans, three or four shirts, and a pair of shoes," Nolan remembered. "That was my wardrobe until Christmas, when I'd get a few more things. My mother would wash and iron my dirty jeans so I'd have a clean pair every day. . . . We had our basic necessities, but most kids want things. But if you wanted 'em, you had to work for 'em."

When the Ryans' eldest daughter entered college the family needed extra money. Lynn Ryan moonlighted as a newspaper carrier for the *Houston Post* and recruited his two sons to help. Nolan was in the second grade when he began rising each morning with his father and brother at 1:00 A.M. They picked up 1,500 papers, drove to a vacant gas station where they folded each and every paper before embarking on the 55-mile route.

Returning home at four or five o'clock in the morning, Nolan crawled into bed to sleep for a few hours before leaving for school. The work was hard, but it taught him a valuable lesson. "The best thing about that job was the sense of responsibility. If you didn't get up, people weren't going to get their paper. They were counting on you."

Nolan began playing Little League baseball at age nine. "Making the Little League team was a thrill for all of us kids in Alvin," he remembered. "When we'd get our caps and uniforms, we'd be so proud, we'd wear the caps to school. . . . We played our games in the Texas heat in those heavy flannel uniforms, but no one seemed to pay the weather any heed."

Playing Little League until he was 13, Nolan made the All-Star team twice and pitched his first no-hitter. Each year, the team started the season with hopes of playing in the Little League World Series in Williamsport, Pennsylvania, but they never made it. Once after his team was defeated in a playoff game, they stood on the field while a speaker addressed them. "One day one of you Little Leaguers will go on to play in the major leagues."

Nolan felt the man was talking about him. He rushed home and exclaimed to his mother, "Mom, that man was talking about me."

"What do you mean?" she asked.

"It's me that he meant, Mom! I'm sure that man was talking about me."

Later Nolan wrote, "I remember that experience as vividly as if it just happened yesterday—the sun, the standing in the field, the man's

In addition to being a standout pitcher, Nolan also starred at basketball for Alvin High School. His all-around ability earned him the Outstanding Athlete Award during his senior year.

voice, his words. I never forgot it. It was a monumental thing in my mind."

By 1963, Nolan was a 6-foot-2-inch, 150-pound sophomore at Alvin High School. One day Red Murff, a scout for the New York Mets, stopped in Alvin to watch a high school tournament. As he sat down, the Alvin coach sent Nolan into the game. Murff watched the gangly kid fire two fastballs and that was enough. "You could hear the ball explode," he recalled. Murff was amazed to learn that Nolan was so young. The next year, Murff sent the following report to the Mets: "Skinny, right-handed junior. Has the best arm I've seen in my life. Could be a real power pitcher someday."

By Nolan's senior year, he had earned a reputation as a wild and intimidating pitcher. In the 1965 district championship game against the Deer Park team, the fear he inspired worked to his advantage. "I hit the first kid up squarely in the helmet and split it," he recalled. "I hit the next guy on the arm and broke it. The third kid went in and begged his coach not to make him hit. That coach assaulted him verbally in front of everybody and shamed him into standing there. . . . I had them after that. If I didn't walk them, I struck them out because they were up there at the edge of the batter's box on their toes, ready to bail out. They were so far from the plate that the inside corner was outside to them. I had no strategy and no finesse. I just kept winging them in there trying to get as close to the plate as possible. They'd forgotten about trying to win the district. They just wanted to go home without any more injuries."

That spring, Red Murff returned to Alvin with Mets head scout Bing Devine. Coach

Watson, unaware that Devine was coming, and upset over two recent losses, put the team through a grueling workout. After pitching batting practice for 30 minutes, Nolan started the game. Exhausted, he pitched miserably; he had no control and his fastball had little movement or velocity. Devine was not impressed. Murff continued to campaign for Nolan, but when the Mets drew up their list of high school players for the 1965 draft, Nolan Ryan was not high on the list. They eventually took him in the 10th round, making him the 295th player chosen overall.

Hurt and disappointed by his low position in the draft, Nolan considered going to college or just getting a full-time job. He was not overjoyed when Murff arrived in Alvin on June 28 with a contract that included a $30,000 signing bonus. Nolan, his parents, and a local sportswriter named Steve Vernon looked over the contract while sitting at the Ryans' kitchen table. Holding a pen and staring at the document, Nolan hesitated. Then he looked across the table at his father. "I could tell he wanted me to sign," Nolan later wrote. "I thought of how I was the last one of the six children he had raised and worked so hard for. I thought of all the hard years of delivering newspapers while most people slept. I thought of the price he had paid doing things for his family."

No one spoke. No one moved. Finally Red Murff said, "Your mom and dad are waiting for you to sign, Nolan. It's on the table."

When Nolan continued to stare at the piece of paper, Vernon leaped up and flung his hands into the air. "What's a matter with you, boy!" he shouted. "You crazy? Sign!"

Startled, Nolan signed.

3

MAKING THE MAJORS

Nolan Ryan's first plane trip landed him in Marion, Virginia, where he joined the Mets rookie league team. The Appalachian League season was already underway. Nolan had to wait until other players were cut from the team before he had a uniform. The biggest size they had barely stretched over his gangly frame. "It was all I could do to keep from showing bare leg between the bottoms of my pants and the tops of my socks," he remembered.

While his teammates dreamed of making it to the big leagues, Ryan thought only of Alvin, Texas. "The only real ambition I had was to see my girlfriend," he said. He had first met Ruth Holdorff in his Little League days, and they had been dating ever since. The highlight of his summer came when Ruth's father brought her to visit the homesick ballplayer. Despite his unhappiness, his fastball crackled. He struck out 115 batters in 78 innings and also led the league with eight hit batsmen. After the season, he went back to Alvin and worked at two jobs, pumping gas and installing air conditioners. Although his signing bonus equaled several years' pay for an average worker, Ryan could not abide idleness. Even when he was earning millions, he found his greatest joy in working hard.

Ryan demonstrates his grip for photographers at the Mets spring training camp in 1967. Though the Mets had high hopes for the young fireballer, an elbow injury forced him to sit out most of the season.

Ryan started the 1966 season at Greenville, South Carolina. "He was the hardest thrower I'd ever seen," recalled his catcher, Duffy Dyer. "He also had a great curve. But he didn't know where either pitch was going. He'd either walk them or strike them out. His fastball just took off. I sat in a half crouch. If he threw it a little bit high I couldn't get there fast enough to stop it, so I made a lot of trips to the backstop." Despite his control problems, Ryan posted a 17-2 record with Greenville, and the Mets called him up to the majors to finish the season.

On September 11, 1966, Ryan made his major league debut against Atlanta. The Braves lineup boasted sluggers such as Hank Aaron, Eddie Mathews, and Joe Torre. "It was frightening," Nolan remembered. "Torre belted a home run off me. Later, Aaron said I had one of the best fastballs he had ever seen." He lost but posted his first three strikeouts in the record book.

The Mets chose Ryan as one of their top 20 prospects and sent him to the instructional league in Winter Haven, Florida. There he met another Mets hopeful, Tom Seaver. "Now there was a guy who had a goal and was focused on it," Ryan said. "I was just there trying to have fun and make a living with a gigantic fastball. Seaver wanted to be an excellent, thinking pitcher." Watching Seaver, Nolan realized he had a lot to learn and a long way to go.

When he joined the Mets AAA Jacksonville, Florida, team in June 1967, Ryan's arm was out of shape. One day he was warming up when he felt a pop in his elbow that turned out to be a torn tendon. Fearing surgery might end his career, Ryan refused treatment and returned to Alvin, hoping that rest would heal the injury.

The single highlight of the season was his marriage to Ruth Holdorff on June 26.

Although his arm still hurt, the young hurler reported to spring training camp in 1968. The press had dubbed him "the new Sandy Koufax," putting pressure on him as never before. A horde of reporters showed up for his first start, against the Dodgers. Ryan faced the leadoff hitter and unleashed a high fastball that was firmly planted in the catcher's mitt when the batter swung. Ryan went three innings that day, not allowing a run or a hit. But his torn tendon flared up again. After that he was inconsistent, missing several starts.

Ryan believed his career was on the line when he took the mound against the defending world champion Cardinals on March 26. Despite his weak arm, he pitched four impressive innings, striking out six. The Mets took him north to New York for the start of the season.

On April 14, 1968, Ryan chalked up his first major league win, a 4–2 victory over the Astros, before his family and friends in Houston. The rookie struck out 7 of the first 10 batters he faced, but blisters on his fingers forced him to leave the game in the seventh inning. Facing the Cincinnati Reds on May 14, he set a Mets record with 14 strikeouts, twice fanning Cincinnati's star catcher Johnny Bench. He blew away five of the last six batters he faced in the 3–2 win.

But problems plagued Ryan during most of the season. He had been drafted by the U.S. Army the previous year; after serving full-time for six months, he was then transferred to the Reserves, which required him to do weekend duty once a month and put in two full weeks during the summer. As a result, he could not

While his teammates relax before a game in May 1968, Ryan soaks his fingers in pickle brine. Ryan had been forced to leave several games because of blisters, and he hoped the brine would toughen the skin on his fingertips.

pitch regularly. Sometimes he missed 10 days between starts, and the disruptions made him inconsistent. Because of the friction caused by gripping the seams when he threw his fastball, blisters formed regularly on the fingers of his pitching hand. He tried an age-old remedy: soaking his fingers in pickle brine. Reporters dubbed him "a dilly of a pitcher."

Not all of his problems were physical. "I really wasn't that far out of high school and hadn't much experience in the world," he later wrote, "but all of a sudden, because of my fastball, I was being compared to Bob Feller and Sandy Koufax. I started out thinking I had to go out there and show them what a good arm I had. I might strike out six or seven the first time through the lineup, but the hitters would realize I was wild and didn't have a breaking ball. Then they would get selective, and I wouldn't make it through the lineup a second time. . . . I realized I was playing right into their hands just because somebody had said something about me and I was trying to live up to it. I wasn't trying to be Nolan Ryan. I was trying to be Feller or Koufax, and nobody can do that."

Because of blisters and his military duty, Ryan missed all of August and finished the season as a reliever. Achieving only a 6-9 record for 1968 despite a low 3.09 ERA, he began to doubt that he could achieve the goal he had set for himself: to stay in the major leagues long enough—five years—to qualify for a pension for the future security of his family.

Since joining the National League in 1962, the Mets had been pathetic. Their first manager, Casey Stengel, claimed they invented new ways to lose. But in 1969, they became the "Amazin' Mets." Trailing the first-place Cubs by 9½ games in August, the talented young team fought back to win 38 of their last 49 games, finishing first in their division. The Mets owed much of their success to a pitching staff starring Tom Seaver, Jerry Koosman, and Gary Gentry. The right-handed Seaver won 25 games and captured the Cy Young Award. Troubled by injuries and blisters, Ryan pitched only 89 innings all season. His contribution was not to come until October, when the Mets squared off against the Atlanta Braves for the National League pennant.

After winning two games in Atlanta, the Mets returned home needing one more win to clinch the flag. Before 53,195 cheering fans at Shea Stadium, they quickly fell behind, 2–0. When Gary Gentry got into trouble in the third inning, manager Gil Hodges beckoned Ryan from the bullpen to face Rico Carty, a .342 hitter, with men on second and third and no one out. Ryan got ahead of Carty, 1-2, and then fired a blazing fastball by him for strike three.

Ryan intentionally walked Orlando Cepeda to load the bases, then smoked a third strike past Clete Boyer. Bob Didier hit a pop fly to end the inning. Ryan went on to pitch seven innings, giving up two runs on three hits, walking two, and striking out seven. The Mets fought back to win the game, 6–4, and went on to upset the favored Baltimore Orioles in the World Series.

Although Ryan made only one appearance during the Series, it was memorable. In Game 3, he earned a save by pitching out of two bases-loaded situations in the late innings. Ryan used his share of the World Series winnings—$18,338—to purchase a 100-acre cattle ranch in Texas.

Ryan's postseason success did not carry over the following year. During the 1970 season, the demands of military duty continued to hurt his consistency. He walked too many batters and

A jubilant Ryan is embraced by Mets catcher Jerry Grote after closing out Game 3 of the 1969 World Series against the Baltimore Orioles. The young fireballer had a modest 6-3 record for the regular season, but two sensational outings in October made him a favorite with Mets fans.

won only two games after June 24, finishing with a 7-11 record. Worse still, his father died of lung cancer. That winter, Ryan considered quitting baseball. His father's death, his dislike of living in New York, and his shaky start and lack of progress had taken their toll on him. But his wife encouraged him to stay with it, and Ryan decided to pitch one more season.

Ryan got off to a strong start in 1971. By June 30, his record stood at 8-4. He had won five consecutive games, walking no more than two hitters in any game. Taking a cue from the popular action movie *Von Ryan's Express*, the press dubbed the pitcher the Ryan Express for his blazing fastball.

Suddenly the Ryan Express derailed. The pitcher lost seven of his next nine starts, giving up 41 walks and 31 runs, and finished with 10 wins and 14 losses. As the Ryans celebrated the birth of their first child, Robert Reid, on November 21, rumors circulated that the Mets were trying to trade their young and erratic pitcher.

On December 18, the Mets sent Ryan and three other players to the California Angels for third baseman Jim Fregosi. The trade came as no surprise to Ryan, but he was dismayed when he read Gil Hodges's comments about him: "Ryan is the starting pitcher that I will miss the least."

"I may not have been an effective big league pitcher yet," said Ryan, "but I sure wanted to make him regret that trade—or at least that comment. Though I still had a lot to learn about pitching, I was a willing student and was eager to do my best for my new team in 1972."

Ryan feeds the livestock on his Texas ranch during the off-season. No matter how much fame and fortune he gained as a ballplayer, Ryan remained a down-to-earth family man with a solid work ethic.

4

A NEW START

T he Angels were rebuilding when Ryan joined the club in 1972. While the Mets had focused on winning, the Angels dedicated themselves to developing talented young players. Ryan began learning about the art of pitching, teaming up with catcher Jeff Torborg in spring training. Both Torborg and Angels pitching coach Tom Morgan immediately noticed problems with Ryan's mechanics and began to work with him. "It was a little like learning to pitch all over again," Ryan recalled. "Pitch after pitch, day after day, I was throwing to Torborg. It was exhausting work, mechanical work, boring at times, but those days turned around my career."

Though Ryan still struggled with his control, he made the All-Star team and finished the season with a 19-16 record and a league-leading 320 strikeouts and 9 shutouts. He also gave up the fewest hits in the league.

During that first year, Ryan discovered the weight room at the Angels ballpark, which was reserved for athletes in other sports. Baseball players had always been discouraged from lifting weights because managers and coaches believed it would make them "musclebound," hampering their ability to swing a bat and throw. But Ryan began to use the workout

Ryan pitches to Kansas City's Amos Otis on May 15, 1973, as the scoreboard shows him only one out away from his first major league no-hitter.

equipment on his own and noticed that he felt looser and more limber as a result. He also rented a house with a swimming pool. Combining swimming with weights, he developed a conditioning routine, focusing much of the work on his upper legs, which provided much of the power for his fastball. Years later Ryan wrote, "There's no doubt in my mind that if it hadn't been for that weight room, I would have been out of the game many years ago. Not only has it helped me prevent injury, but it's also kept me strong so I could continue to hold up over the long grind." In his first three years with the Angels, Ryan pitched more than 1,000 innings, a workload unmatched since by any pitcher.

In 1973 the Angels boosted Ryan's salary to $54,000, doubling his previous year's pay. He showed his gratitude by pitching his first no-hitter on May 15, and exactly two months later he pitched his second. He became a 20-game winner for the first time, with a 21-16 record.

In an attempt to measure just how fast Ryan's fastball traveled, the Angels asked scientists from Rockwell International, a leading technology company, to clock his pitches during a game, using the most advanced devices of the time. Up to this point, the accepted record had been 98.6 miles per hour, set by Bob Feller in 1946. That night, Ryan was clocked at 100.9 miles per hour. But Ryan always believed—and many batters agreed—that he had thrown faster pitches than any he unleashed in that game.

Numbers cannot really describe the experience of facing Ryan. Not even the verbally gifted Reggie Jackson could put it into words: "One thing that I wish I was able to do was to explain to people how hard he threw. . . . If I could just stand you up at the plate and let you listen or watch, it would be the eighth or ninth wonder of the world to you. The average person just couldn't appreciate what [Nolan] was doing."

Ryan won a career-high 22 games in 1974, the last time he would reach the 20-win circle. His 367 strikeouts again led the league. The following year, nagging injuries plagued him, but they were temporarily forgotten on June 1 when he threw his fourth no-hitter, blanking Baltimore 1–0 and tying Sandy Koufax's record. It was the first of his no-hitters that was witnessed by his wife, Ruth.

In August 1975, when Ryan's record was 14-12, he underwent surgery to remove bone chips from his pitching elbow. Following the no-hitter, the chips had become a chronic problem. He lost eight games in a row. "I had gone from being a dominating pitcher to one the hitters couldn't wait to face," he said. The press suddenly attacked their former golden boy, calling him lazy and accusing him of giving up. Stung by their cruelty, Ryan reacted by refusing to talk to the media.

He looked forward to the off-season, as he and Ruth awaited the birth of their second child in January. To honor Nolan's friend and coach Jimmy Reese, the Ryans named their second son Nolan Reese Ryan and always called the boy Reese. A year later the Ryans celebrated the birth of a daughter, Wendy Lynn.

Ryan silenced the critics by making a comeback in 1976, leading the league with seven shutouts and striking out 327 hitters in 284 innings. Impressed by his performance, the Angels signed him to a three-year contract at $300,000 a year. In 1977 he led the American

Ryan relaxes at his Alvin, Texas, home with his wife, Ruth, and his children Reese (left) and Wendy, in 1979. Eager to spend more time with his family during the baseball season, Ryan soon left the Angels and signed with the Houston Astros as a free agent.

League in strikeouts (327) for the fifth time in six years. The *Sporting News* named the 30-year-old hurler the American League pitcher of the year.

A series of nagging injuries assailed Ryan in 1978. He missed several starts and finished the season with a 10-13 record. Despite his disappointing performance, he once again led the American League in strikeouts, ending the year eighth on the all-time list of career strikeouts.

Early in 1979, the Ryans' son Reid, age 7,

was struck by a car, suffering severe internal injuries. Wanting to be with his family, Ryan spent as much time at home as possible, joining the team on the road only one day before he was scheduled to pitch. Despite the difficult circumstances, he ended the year at 16-14 with 17 complete games, 5 shutouts, and an average of a strikeout an inning for 223 innings.

After the season, Ryan was eligible to become a free agent. He talked to Angels general manager Buzzie Bavasi about a contract extension, but Bavasi balked at Ryan's request for $500,000 a year for two years and $700,000 for a third year. "Why should I pay that much for a 16-14 pitcher?" Bavasi said, in a statement he came to regret. "I can get two 8-7 pitchers for less."

When Ryan's agent, Dick Moss, put out feelers, the Yankees offered to pay $1 million a year. But Ryan did not want to move his family back to New York City. When the Houston Astros offered to match the Yankees' bid, Ryan jumped at the opportunity to play baseball a half hour from his home in Alvin. The Ryan Express was Texas bound.

5

HOMECOMING

When Nolan Ryan signed a three-year contract with Houston for $1 million a year in 1979, he believed it would be his last. He would be 35 when the contract was up. He had financial security and was ready to settle in and finish his career in his home state.

The Houston Astrodome had artificial turf, which Ryan did not like; but he liked the big outfield, the controlled temperature, and the roof that guaranteed that none of his starts would ever be interrupted by a rain delay. The Astrodome also housed the most complete array of workout equipment he had ever seen. Aided by Dr. A. Eugene Coleman, the Astros' instructor of strength and conditioning, Ryan developed the most regimented and rigorous training program ever followed by a baseball player. Even after pitching a no-hitter or striking out 19 batters, he would excuse himself from the cameramen, reporters, and well-wishers and do his postgame routine on the stationary bike.

Ryan's hopes were high when the 1980 season began. Despite his slow start, the Astros came within one game of making it to their first World Series. In an exciting National League Championship Series against the

Making his first start for the Astros, Ryan does the unexpected by hitting his first major league home run, a three-run blast against the Los Angeles Dodgers. He had little chance to perfect his home run trot, however, because he hit only one more round-tripper during the rest of his career.

Phillies—four of the five games were settled in extra innings—Ryan got two starts but was unable to stop a powerful Phillies lineup that included such all-time greats as Pete Rose and Mike Schmidt.

The next year the Astros came close again, but Ryan lost the deciding game of the split-season Western Division playoff to the Dodgers, 4–0. The 1981 season proved far more costly to him in another way. A players' strike cut 52 days out of the schedule, costing Ryan $300,000 of his salary. Although he lost more money in the strike than any other player, he supported the Players' Association. "I realized I would never have been in the position to lose that money if it had not been for the effort of the association and the players who went before me," he said. Few players had earned as much as $100,000 when he had broken in in 1966.

Ryan was still the dominant power pitcher in baseball. Often he went into the seventh or eighth inning of a game with a no-hitter in progress; he would throw a record 12 one-hitters in his career. "Don't let him smell a no-hitter in the sixes and sevens," said Chili Davis of the San Francisco Giants, "because then he gets really tough."

However, Ryan had gone six years without actually completing a no-hitter. He was now 34, an age considered close to antiquity for a pitcher. Then, on September 26, 1981, before a sellout crowd in a nationally televised game against the Dodgers at the Astrodome, he locked into perfect control of his curve, which set up the hitters for his fastball, and he became the first man to notch five no-hitters, toppling another Koufax record.

Phil Garner was the Astros' second baseman that day. "Most no-hitters sort of develop as they go along. Not Nolan's. He would be overpowering from the start. You knew from the first pitch that this guy was going to be unhittable. . . . You'd say to yourself, 'My God, he's going to throw a no-hitter tonight. I better be ready. The ball that I don't catch may be the only hit he gives up.' "

By 1983, Ryan was closing in on Hall of Famer Walter Johnson's career strikeout record of 3,508. Illness and injuries kept him from starting the season on time, but in his third start, on April 27 at Montreal, he rang up victim number 3,509. Though he had once thought of retiring at the age of 35, he now forgot all about it.

The Astros were a mediocre team for the next few years. Toiling faithfully in spite of the team's shortcomings, Ryan reached the age of 39 but amazingly lost nothing off his fastball. On July 11, 1985, he became the first pitcher in history to reach 4,000 strikeouts. But he was no longer among the National League strikeout leaders; young stars such as Dwight Gooden of the Mets and Ryan's teammate Mike Scott rose to the fore. His innings pitched slipped below 200 as his complete games dwindled.

The Astros surprised the experts by winning the National League West in 1986, but once again a chance for a World Series start eluded Ryan, who had pitched all year with pain in his elbow. It was hurting when he started Game 5 of the National League Championship Series against the Mets. In the fourth inning he went into second base standing up instead of sliding and fractured his heel. Pitching brilliantly through the pain in his elbow and foot, he left

For many years, baseball fans thought that the great Walter Johnson's record of 3,508 career strikeouts would stand forever. However, Ryan shattered the mark on April 27, 1983, and went on to exceed Johnson by more than 2,000 strikeouts.

Ryan delivers a curve ball to the Mets' Len Dykstra to start Game 2 of the 1986 National League playoff. Ryan did everything possible to defeat his former team, but the Mets captured a hard-fought series and went on to win the world championship.

after nine innings with the game tied, 1–1. The Mets won in the 12th, 2–1, going on to capture the pennant and the World Series.

Without consulting Ryan, the Astros' front office ordered a 115-pitch limit on all his starts in 1987, no matter what the situation was in the game. Ryan objected; he felt fine physically and saw no reason for the team to protect him. He was still throwing above 90 miles per hour, with more consistent control of his curve and change-up, and he was working the batters more effectively. Despite the 115-pitch limit, he led the league with 270 strikeouts, averaging a record 11.48 per 9 innings, and turned in the best ERA, 2.76. But he was unable to pitch a single com-

plete game for the first time since his brief debut in 1966. The Astros' lack of hitting and the team's poor relief pitching combined to saddle Ryan with an 8-16 won-lost record. In every other respect he turned in a Cy Young Award season.

By 1988, Ryan was still earning $1 million a year, while other players had soared into the multimillion-dollar brackets. That did not bother Ryan, but when the Astros tried to cut his pay for the 1989 season, he concluded that they were not really interested in keeping him. Though he knew he could do a lot better in the free-agent marketplace, Ryan had no desire to leave Houston. He let the Astros know that he would be happy to stay at his current salary, but they told him to take the pay cut or leave.

The Texas Rangers, just a few hundred miles down the road in Arlington, never really believed the Astros would let Ryan get away. But just in case, Texas general manager Tom Grieve called Ryan's agent and asked if Ryan would consider signing with the Rangers. Ryan replied, "I'm a diehard Texan, and I want to remain in Texas." Not surprisingly, so did Ruth, Reid, Reese, and Wendy Ryan. And so on December 7, 1988, Nolan Ryan became a Ranger.

6

RYAN TO
THE RESCUE

When 42-year-old Nolan Ryan joined the Texas Rangers in 1989, they were a floundering club with a troubled history. Since moving from Washington, D.C., in 1972, they had never won a division title. They had finished sixth or seventh in four of the past five years, losing 91 games in 1988. Their ownership kept shifting like a Texas tumbleweed blowing in the wind. In the baseball world, the Arlington franchise was viewed as a ragtag organization.

Signing Nolan Ryan gave the team instant credibility. The owners and fans expected Ryan to save the franchise, and he did all anybody could ask of him to achieve these goals. He won 16 games, his highest total in seven years; five times he took no-hitters into the eighth or ninth inning. More records fell: he topped 300 strikeouts for the sixth time; and on August 22, he matched the 101-degree Texas heat by firing a 96-mile-an-hour fastball past Oakland's Rickey Henderson for strikeout number 5,000.

After 21 years, Ryan suddenly became a legend. Companies seeking commercial endorsements lined up like autograph seekers: Whataburger, Wrangler Jeans, Biz Mart, Southwest Airlines, Bic Shavers, Justin Boots, and Advil. He seemed to be pitching more products on television than fastballs

Ryan meets the press after signing as a free agent with the Texas Rangers in December 1988. Though Ryan was approaching his 42nd birthday, he went on to win 47 games for the Rangers over the next five seasons.

on the mound. The media searched for adjectives to describe his amazing feats. But Ryan took it all in stride, attributing his success to nothing but hard work. "People think I roll up to the ballpark at seven o'clock for a 7:30 game and hang around for two or three hours and leave," he said. "I spend eight to nine hours a day at the stadium, every day, for seven months of the year."

Ryan devoted many of those hours to a conditioning routine of his own design. Following a game, he iced his pitching arm and rode the Lifecycle for 30 minutes. The next morning he worked out with a weight machine and dumbbells for upper and lower body strength. In the afternoon he worked on his abdominal muscles for 40 minutes, using 15 varieties of lifts, crunches, and sit-ups, followed by a 20-minute light dumbbell program. Then he ran 40-yard sprints forward and backward, threw a football and baseball, and topped it all off with another session on the stationary bicycle or a swim.

As Ryan's popularity grew, so did the demands of the fans. Crowds mobbed him everywhere he went. Ryan was always one of the few players who would come out of the ballpark late at night after a game and begin signing autographs while his teammates called to him from the team bus. More than once he would tell the team to go ahead, and he would take a cab to the hotel. He only balked at signing multiple items for people who were obviously in the business of buying and selling baseball memorabilia.

In the winter, the Rangers would bring truckloads of mail and photos to Ryan's home, and he would spend an hour each day, sometimes

longer, answering the letters and signing photos. Unlike some players, who would accumulate boxes of fan mail during the season and then throw it all away, he vowed to answer every one of the 300 to 400 letters he received each day. And he would not let anyone else sign autographs for him.

When Ryan signed with the Rangers for the 1990 season, he expected the contract to be the last of his career. For the first time, he began a season shooting for a specific stat: he was 11 short of 300 wins. At the age of 43, Ryan was throwing the kind of smoke pitchers half his age wished they could command. His fastball regis-

Ryan fans Rickey Henderson of the Oakland A's on August 22, 1989, chalking up his 5,000th career strikeout. He finished the season with a league-leading 301 strikeouts and a solid 16-10 record.

Beginning his 26th major league season, Ryan signs autographs at the Rangers' 1992 spring training camp. Despite his enormous celebrity and the many demands on his time, Ryan was always gracious to fans. "I'm no better than anyone else," he insisted.

tering in the mid-90s, he fanned 16 White Sox in his 12th and final one-hitter on April 26. He was 4-0 by mid-May, but despite his superb conditioning, his back began to hurt. He spent three weeks on the disabled list while the newspapers, unable to chart his strikeouts, published diagrams of his spine, showing the stress fracture that doctors had discovered.

Despite the continuing soreness in his back, Ryan was back on the mound in Oakland on July 11, with his wife and daughter in the stands and his son Reese serving as batboy in the Rangers dugout. He had a new catcher, John

Russell, whom he had never pitched to. Lacking the usual mustard on his fastball, he relied mostly on his curve, which was behaving perfectly. By the fifth inning, he was "smelling" another no-hitter. While the teams were changing sides, first-base umpire Durwood Merrill said to Don Denkinger, working behind the plate, "Don, he's going to pitch a no-hitter. They're not going to get him. Look at the fire. Look at the intensity in those eyes."

After every inning, Reese Ryan massaged his father's back as hard as he could. "Come on, Dad, you can do it," he urged. And he did do it, completing his sixth no-hitter, a 5–0 victory. Nine years had passed since Ryan's fifth, and 17 years since his first. Throughout the rest of the season, Ryan continued to pitch in pain, but his rigorous conditioning program had strengthened his muscles enough to get him through. On the nights when both his fastball and curve were working, he was unhittable. The first time Chicago White Sox superstar Frank Thomas faced Ryan, he struck out four times.

Ryan won his 299th game on July 20 at home against Detroit, and his 300th came on July 31 at Milwaukee. His only regret was that he had reached the milestone on the road. After the game, he told the press that he had been "wishing that I could do something meaningful at Arlington Stadium. Those fans had made my last two years so special that I felt I owed it to them." He then left the mob of reporters and put in 30 minutes on the stationary bike, preparing for his next start.

7

THE INTIMIDATOR

Nolan Ryan never won a Cy Young Award, never led the league in wins, and won more than 20 games just twice. But for more than 20 years he was the most dominating, awesome, fear-inspiring pitcher in baseball. In the mold of Hall of Fame fireballers of the past, such as Walter Johnson and Lefty Grove, Ryan was—through-out two decades and part of another—the Intimidator.

The friendly, soft-spoken, easygoing cattle rancher from Texas was a different man on the pitching mound, the place he called his "office." "In the big leagues," Ryan explained, "you have to be single-minded, focused, and really tough. You've got to go after the hitters, take every advantage you can, work on their weak spots, and want to beat them. . . . Anybody who's been on a big league mound knows that you're always one pitch from failure."

Fear was a powerful weapon in Ryan's arse-nal. The very prospect of facing him caused many a player to wish for a pulled muscle or a high fever. "What stands out in my mind," recalled Frank White of the Kansas City Royals, "is the first time you saw him throwing on the sidelines and how hard he threw the ball. I remember how I had to really muster up enough

Unleashing his booming fastball, Ryan shows the gritty determination that drove him through 27 big league seasons. Though a genial, soft-spoken person off the field, Ryan was a merciless competitor once he stepped onto the pitcher's mound.

47

courage to go up there and face that fastball. I had to overcome being afraid, and my knees were knocking. Then I thought, I'm not going to let him strike me out." Ryan got White twice that day. Veteran major leaguer Oscar Gamble added, "A good night against Ryan is 0 for 4 and don't get hit in the head."

Ryan did not like batters bunting on him and did everything he could do to discourage it. Harold Reynolds was a speedy infielder with Seattle when Ryan came to the Rangers in 1989. "The word was that you don't bunt on Nolan because he might hit you with the pitch," Reynolds said. "He knew I liked to bunt and about the second or third time I faced him, it was a bunt situation. When I stepped into the batter's box he came part way down from the mound toward me and looked me in the eye and said, 'Don't even think about it.' I was shivering. I mean quaking in my shoes, all but saying, 'Okay, okay.' And I never bunted on him."

Those who tried it often put their lives on the line. One such attempt remained an indelible memory for pitcher Claude Osteen. "One day I squared away to bunt and I was facing him directly, and he threw one that had me right in the heart and somehow I either had to get the bat up in front of me so the ball hits the handle or I'd probably die. I don't know how I did it, but the ball hit my bat and the bat just disintegrated. That scared me a little bit."

As much as hitters love to hit home runs (Ryan gave up 322 of them), taking Ryan deep was not a total joy. "If you hit a home run against him," said veteran third baseman Mike Pagliarulo, "you kept your head down and went a little faster around the bases. You didn't go slow, didn't show him up. Next time up you didn't stand there and dig in at the plate. You didn't mind doing that to other pitchers, but not to Ryan, because one of his weapons was his intimidation, and he was going to be the intimidator out there and make you pay."

By the time Ryan joined the Rangers, he was old enough to be the father of many of the players in the clubhouse. He was also pitching against more and more hitters who had grown up idolizing him. Many of them, like Detroit slugger Cecil Fielder, were awestruck when they stepped up to bat against the seemingly ageless king of the hill. "When I was growing up in California, I would go and watch him pitch," Fielder said. "We all looked up to him. And then all of a sudden I'm facing him in the batter's box and he's pitching the ball to me. For the first couple of times I was not concentrating because I was thinking, 'That's Nolan Ryan out there trying to get me out.' That was one of the greatest thrills of my career, a sort of nervous thrill."

8

A LIVING LEGEND

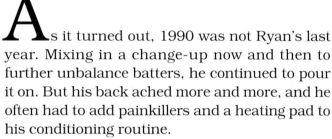

As it turned out, 1990 was not Ryan's last year. Mixing in a change-up now and then to further unbalance batters, he continued to pour it on. But his back ached more and more, and he often had to add painkillers and a heating pad to his conditioning routine.

Warming up in Arlington for a start against the Toronto Blue Jays on May 1, 1991, Ryan told Rangers pitching coach Tom House, "I feel old today. My back hurts, my finger hurts, my ankle hurts, everything hurts." Then, with 33,549 people cheering him on, he went out and threw his seventh career no-hitter. After the game he said, "I think that this no-hitter is the most rewarding because it was in front of these hometown fans who have supported me since I have been here. This one was for them."

A streaky 1992 season—he lost three in a row, then won five in a row, and then lost his last six decisions—and recurring minor injuries prompted Ryan to announce on February 11, 1993, that the coming season would be his last.

Exulting in triumph, Ryan is carried off the field by his Texas teammates after pitching his seventh career no-hitter, on May 1, 1991.

During spring training, so many fans clamored for Ryan's autograph that the Rangers had to post a sign every morning informing fans of when the pitcher would be available. When he appeared, he would sign everything put in front of him for hours. His mail averaged 500 letters a day.

At every stop around the league Ryan held a special press conference, reflecting on his career accomplishments and future plans. From a baseball point of view, Ryan endured a frustrating season, as a variety of injuries kept him out of the rotation for long stretches of time. Reporters were not surprised by his reply when he was asked in midseason if he would reconsider his retirement. "No," he said, "my body is telling me it's time to quit."

Despite Ryan's sparse contributions, the Rangers stayed in the thick of the fight for the American League Western Division title. On August 4, the Rangers were playing the league-leading White Sox in Chicago when Ryan hit Chicago third baseman Robin Ventura with a pitch. Enraged, Ventura charged the mound. Ryan stood his ground and greeted Ventura with a series of rights to the head. Both players began to wrestle on the ground as the dugouts emptied and the umpires rushed in to restore order. It did not matter to Ryan that Ventura was 20 years younger.

"Nolan just collected himself like nothing happened and went on to retire 17 of the next 18," recalled his admiring manager, Kevin Kennedy. "I think the incident pumped us up so much we went on to take that series and maintain our drive in the pennant race. It was like the hero came to the rescue, at a time when we needed it." Despite

Ryan's inspiration, the Rangers finished second to the White Sox, ending Ryan's last chance for a possible World Series start.

Ryan was looking forward to throwing his last fastball before the hometown fans, but that was not fated to be. On September 22, he was in Seattle warming up for a start against the Mariners when he experienced pain and tightness in his elbow. Determined to throw as hard

Ryan ices his elbow after pitching against his son Reid in a 1991 exhibition game. Despite a variety of aches and pains, the elder Ryan won 12 games during the regular season, posting an excellent 2.91 earned-run average.

as he could no matter what, he started the game throwing what one batter described as a "104-mile-an-hour fastball with hair on it." But he was as wild as he had been in his rookie year, walking three in a row after giving up a leadoff single. Then Dann Howitt, a .211 hitter, sliced an opposite-field grand slam. Ryan threw two balls to the next batter, Dave Magadan. As he delivered the third pitch, he heard a popping sound and felt a burning sensation in his elbow. "I knew I was done," he said later. Ryan tried to throw one more pitch despite the pain in his arm, but the ball had nothing on it, and he walked off the mound with a torn ligament as Magadan took first base. It was a sad way to end what had become a nightmarish farewell season, but it was Ryan's nature to take frustration and failure in his stride, the same way he had handled his many successes. His last game would be the least of the memories that players and fans would carry with them, except perhaps for Dann Howitt, who will remain forever the last man to get a hit off Nolan Ryan.

"He pitched his heart out," said Seattle slugger Ken Griffey, Jr., after the game. "He didn't give in to you, and that's the way a pitcher's supposed to be. I think up until the last pitch he threw, he didn't give in."

On the last day of the season in Arlington Ryan was on the field in uniform, though he was unable to pitch. Before the game, he went to home plate to exchange the lineup cards with Kansas City great George Brett, who was also suiting up as an active player for the last time. The great strikeout pitcher and the perennial .300 hitter, who had enjoyed the challenge of squaring off against each other over the years,

were slated to see each other again at the Hall of Fame induction ceremonies in 1999.

Over a phenomenal 27-year career, Ryan had averaged more than one strikeout per inning through 5,387 innings pitched. He retired with his name on 53 major league records. Unlike many players, who find it difficult to adjust to ordinary life after a career of heroics, Ryan simply applied his tremendous work ethic to other pursuits. In addition to a

Never one to back down from a confrontation, the 47-year-old Ryan takes on Chicago's Robin Ventura during an August 4, 1993, contest at Arlington Stadium. Ventura had unwisely charged the mound after being hit by one of Ryan's deliveries.

long-term contract with the Rangers that called for Ryan to make personal appearances and coach young pitchers in the minors, Ryan kept himself busy overseeing his investments, which included four ranches and two banks. He also worked with his sons' high school and college baseball teams.

Ryan once described himself as a "country kid from Texas with the ability to throw a ball and the dedication to keep himself in shape. I love the cheers and the applause and I am grateful people come out to watch me pitch. I even appreciate that people like to see me in person and talk to me and get my autograph. But I'm just a man. I'm no better than anybody else, even if I have an unusual and marketable talent."

Despite his modesty, the impression Ryan made on baseball players and officials in the game was as lasting as his impact on the record book. Sparky Anderson, one of the most successful managers in baseball history, called Ryan "the only national hero in baseball. People don't understand what he has had to go through to stay on top through three decades. He's the most amazing specimen we've had. He might have pitched until he was 50 if he hadn't hurt his arm."

Luis Mayoral, an executive with the Rangers, knew all the greats of the game during the years of Ryan's career. "What I admire most about Nolan," he said, "is not a particular game, but the way he carries himself. A baseball giant, with all the records and the money, he still, until his final day, worked more than anyone on the club to stay in shape. He was very aware of what he meant to the fans, so whenever possible he made himself available to them. Nowadays, with the millions players are making, they get lost in all the 'earthly glory.' But not Nolan Ryan. That's what I most remember about him. Not the curve, not the fastball, not the no-hitters, not the 5,000-plus strikeouts, but the type of man he is."

Lou Whitaker, the veteran infielder of the Detroit Tigers, who faced many Ryan heaters through the years, summed up the pitcher's legacy in a single sentence: "It will be a pretty long time before we see another Nolan Ryan."

CHRONOLOGY

1947   Born Lynn Nolan Ryan, Jr., in Refugio, Texas, on January 31

1963   Discovered by New York Mets scout Red Murff while pitching for the Alvin High School team

1965   Signs professional contract with New York Mets; makes professional debut with Marion in the Appalachian League

1966   Named Western Carolinas pitcher of the year after posting 17-2 record at Greenville; strikes out 35 batters in 19 innings at Williamsport; makes major league debut against Atlanta Braves on September 11

1967   Sits out most of season with elbow injury; marries Ruth Holdorff on June 26

1968   Pitches first full season with the Mets, posting a 6-9 record

1969   Goes 6-3 in limited action with the Mets but wins a crucial game in the playoffs and earns a save in the World Series

1971   Mets trade Ryan to California Angels

1972   Ryan leads American League with 320 strikeouts and 9 shutouts and is named to the All-Star team

1973   Enjoys first 20-win season and pitches two no-hitters; ends season with 383 strikeouts, setting a new major league record

1974   Wins career-high 22 games; leads league with 367 strikeouts; pitches third and fourth no-hitters

1979   Signs with Houston Astros as free agent

1981   Pitches fifth career no-hitter, setting new major league record

1983   Records 3,509th career strikeout, breaking major league mark held by Walter Johnson

1985   Becomes first pitcher in history to record 4,000 strikeouts

1989   Joins Texas Rangers as a free agent; enjoys sixth 300-strikeout season and records 5,000th career strikeout

1990   Pitches sixth career no-hitter and wins 300th game

1991   Notches seventh and last no-hitter

1993   Pitches 27th and final season in the major leagues; retires with 5,714 strikeouts and 52 additional major league records

MAJOR LEAGUE STATISTICS

NEW YORK METS, CALIFORNIA ANGELS, HOUSTON ASTROS, TEXAS RANGERS

YEAR	TEAM	W	L	ERA	G	GS	CG	SHO	SV	IP	H	R	ER	BB	SO
1966	NY N	0	1	15.00	2	1	0	0	0	3.0	5	5	5	3	6
1968		6	9	3.09	21	18	3	0	0	134.0	93	50	46	75	133
1969		6	3	3.53	25	10	2	0	1	89.1	60	38	35	53	92
1970		7	11	3.41	27	19	5	2	1	132.0	86	59	50	97	125
1971		10	14	3.97	30	26	3	0	0	152.0	125	78	67	116	137
1972	CAL A	19	16	2.28	39	39	20	*9	0	284.0	166	80	72	*157	*329
1973		21	16	2.87	41	39	26	4	1	326.0	238	113	104	*162	*383
1974		22	16	2.89	42	41	26	3	0	*333.0	221	127	107	*202	*367
1975		14	12	3.45	28	28	10	5	0	198.0	152	90	76	132	*186
1976		17	*18	3.36	39	39	21	*7	0	284.0	193	117	106	*183	*327
1977		19	16	2.77	37	37	22	4	0	299.0	198	110	92	*204	*341
1978		10	13	3.71	31	31	14	3	0	235.0	183	106	97	*148	*260
1979		16	14	3.59	34	34	17	5	0	223.0	169	104	89	114	*223
1980	HOU N	11	10	3.35	35	35	4	2	0	234.0	205	100	87	*98	200
1981		11	5	*1.69	21	21	5	3	0	149.0	99	34	28	68	140
1982		16	12	3.16	35	35	10	3	0	250.1	196	100	88	*109	245
1983		14	9	2.98	29	29	5	2	0	196.1	134	74	65	101	183
1984		12	11	3.04	30	30	5	2	0	183.2	143	78	62	69	197
1985		10	12	3.80	35	35	4	0	0	232.0	205	108	98	95	209
1986		12	8	3.34	30	30	1	0	0	178.0	119	72	66	82	194
1987		8	16	*2.76	34	34	0	0	0	211.2	154	75	65	87	*270
1988		12	11	3.52	33	33	4	1	0	220.0	186	98	86	87	*228
1989	TX A	16	10	3.20	32	32	6	2	0	239.1	162	96	85	98	*301
1990		13	9	3.44	30	30	5	2	0	204.0	137	86	78	74	*232
1991		12	6	2.91	27	27	2	2	0	173.0	102	58	56	72	203
1992		5	9	3.72	27	27	2	0	0	157.1	138	75	65	69	157
1993		5	5	4.88	13	13	0	0	0	66.1	54	47	36	40	46
Totals		324	292	3.19	807	773	222	61	3	5385.0	3923	2178	1911	2795	5714

Hitting Totals

AVG	AB	H	HR	RBI
.110	852	94	2	33

†**Led League**

FURTHER READING

Lace, W. W. *Sports Great: Nolan Ryan.* Hillside, NJ: Enslow Publishing, 1993.

Rappoport, Ken. *Nolan Ryan: The Ryan Express.* New York: Dillon Press, 1992.

Ryan, Nolan. *Miracle Man: Nolan Ryan, The Autobiography.* Irving, TX: Word, 1992.

Ryan, Nolan, et al. *Pitching and Hitting.* Englewood Cliffs, NJ: Prentice Hall, 1982.

Ryan, Nolan, and Harvey Frommer. *Throwing Heat: The Autobiography of Nolan Ryan.* New York: Doubleday, 1988.

Ryan, Nolan, and Mickey Hershkowitz. *Kings of the Hill: An Irreverent Look at the Men on the Mound.* New York: HarperCollins, 1992.

Ryan, Nolan, and Tom House (with Jim Rosenthal). *The Pitcher's Bible: The Ultimate Guide to Power, Precision, and Long-Term Performance.* New York: Simon & Schuster, 1991.

INDEX

PICTURE CREDITS
National Baseball Library and Archive, Cooperstown, NY: pp. 11, 14, 18, 20, 24, 60; UPI/Bettmann: pp. 2, 8–9, 13, 25, 26, 28, 31, 32, 34, 36, 38, 40, 44, 47, 48, 50, 53, 56, 58.

LOIS P. NICHOLSON holds a bachelor of science degree in elementary education and a master's degree in education from Salisbury State University. She has worked as a school librarian in both an elementary and a middle school in Rock Hill, Maryland. She has also written *Cal Ripken, Jr.: Quiet Hero* (Tidewater, 1993) and biographies of George Washington Carver, Michael Jackson, Oprah Winfrey and Casey Stengel for Chelsea House.

JIM MURRAY, veteran sports columnist of the *Los Angeles Times,* is one of America's most acclaimed writers. He has been named "America's Best Sportswriter" by the National Association of Sportscasters and Sportswriters 14 times, was awarded the Red Smith Award, and was twice winner of the National Headliner Award. In addition, he was awarded the J. Taylor Spink Award in 1987 for "meritorious contributions to baseball writing." With this award came his 1988 induction into the National Baseball Hall of Fame in Cooperstown, New York. In 1990, Jim Murray was awarded the Pulitzer Prize for Commentary.

EARL WEAVER is the winningest manager in Baltimore Orioles history by a wide margin. He compiled 1,480 victories in his 17 years at the helm. After managing eight different minor league teams, he was given the chance to lead the Orioles in 1968. Under his leadership the Orioles finished lower than second place in the American League East only four times in 17 years. One of only 12 managers in big league history to have managed in four or more World Series, Earl was named Manager of the Year in 1979. The popular Weaver had his number 5 retired in 1982, joining Brooks Robinson, Frank Robinson, and Jim Palmer, whose numbers were retired previously. Earl Weaver continues his association with the professional baseball scene by writing, broadcasting, and coaching.